THE DENGINEERS

BUILD YOUR DREAM

DEN

D0488230

STUDIO PRESS

Written by Laura Baker
Illustrated by Ian Upstone
Designed by Claire Munday
Edited by Emma Drage

Printed in China
1 3 5 7 9 10 8 6 4 2

First published in 2019 by Studio Press Books
an imprint of Bonnier Books UK
The Plaza, 535 King's Road, London, SW10 0SZ
www.studiopressbooks.co.uk
www.bonnierbooks.co.uk

By arrangement with the BBC
The BBC and CBBC logos are trademarks of the British
Broadcasting Corporation and are used under licence
BBC logo © BBC 1996 CBBC logo © BBC 2015

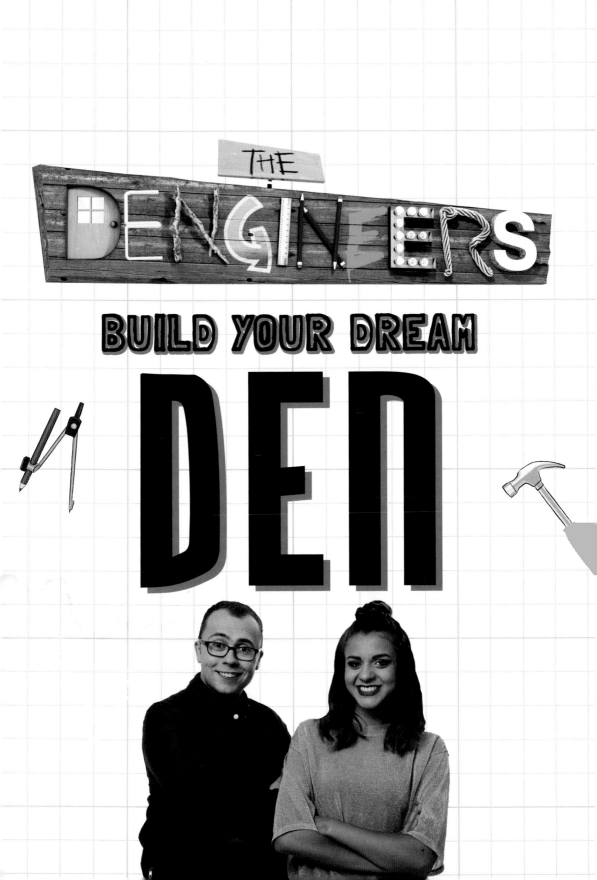

CONTENTS

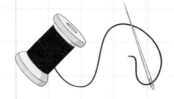

We're excited to welcome you to the very first *Dengineers* book! We hope it will help you to create your own dream den.

Making dens is our favourite thing to do. We love everything about them, from the planning to the designing to the building. Whether you're just starting out or have designed dens before, this book can help you with your unique den creations. With advice and information from your favourite *Dengineers* designers, you will see how easy it is to get started and how you can take inspiration from the world around you.

We've had a huge variety of den themes on *The Dengineers*, from retro railway to modern DJ to Hawaiian beach hut! Each den has had its own unique look, including a night sky observatory and a mini sports stadium. We even created our very own Scottish castle! We love making dens that deliver exactly what our young Dengineers want.

That should be the same for you too – remember that your dream den is all about YOU! Think about your favourite things, your hobbies and what you want to do in your den. It can be your private retreat or a place to share with your friends. It can be calm and quiet or noisy and fun. If you design a den that's all about you, it will be truly individual!

And don't worry if you're not a pro at drawing or building. The most important part of den creation is having the ideas and making them work for you. So get planning, get designing and get creating. Let your imagination run wild, have fun and don't stop until YOUR DEN IS DONE!

Love from, *The Dengineers* team

Join presenters Lauren and Joe
as you go on an adventure to
build your very own dream den.

INTRODUCTION

A den is a special place just for you. It can be big and complex or small and simple. Either way, it is YOUR dream space, where you can escape and be yourself.

DENGINEERS ONLY!

In this book, we'll show you how to make both indoor and outdoor dens using materials and spaces you have around the house.

The first section of the book gives you steps for basic starter dens, how to build upon these structures, and tools you'll need for the design process.

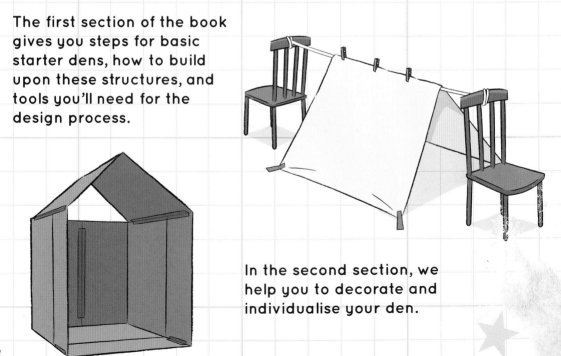

In the second section, we help you to decorate and individualise your den.

In this book there are 16 brilliant den themes to suit whatever your passion may be: adventure, dance, reading, cinema, sport and more!

Inspired by dens built on the programme, each theme is packed full of suggestions for how to make your own version at home.

Just remember to ask for an adult's permission before you get started, and make sure they are always on hand to help you with any building activities (see our safety tips on page 13). The activities throughout the book also mention when adult help is needed.

Now put on your Dengineering overalls, gather your supplies... and get started!

MEET THE DENGINEERS

This team of super-talented designers and architects create top-notch dens on *The Dengineers* programme. Look out for their tips throughout the book!

THE DESIGNERS

SEGE

'Sege the Lege' has over 30 years of building experience. He runs his own construction company and is a legend when it comes to creating unique builds.

MARAL

Maral has been named a role model in British architecture. She loves to bring people's stories into the buildings she designs for them.

EMMA

Emma is an interior designer with a special talent for finding just the right fabrics and patterns. She is obsessed with colour!

TONY & SATWINDER

Tony runs his own architecture company and works with kids to get them building. Satwinder teaches architecture at a university and, like Maral, has been named a role model in British architecture. Tony and Satwinder work as a duo on *The Dengineers* to design dream dens.

THE PRESENTERS

LAUREN

Lauren is a CBBC television presenter and has been with *The Dengineers* since the beginning. She isn't afraid to help out with den building when needed.

JOE

Joe joined *The Dengineers* as a presenter in season three. He loves travelling around the country meeting new families and building amazing dens.

GETTING STARTED

To get started on your den-building adventure, you need to find a space for your den. This could be inside or outside, permanent or temporary. It just needs to be somewhere with enough space for you! And then, of course, you need to build the basic den structure. Check out the suggestions in this section for various den types that you could create, all using materials you can find at home.

STEPS FOR BUILDING A DREAM DEN:

1 Find the perfect space for your den.

2 Choose the type of den you want to build.

3 Pick a theme for your den.

4 Make a mood board for your theme.

5 Sketch out your plans.

6 Gather your materials.

7 Get building!

DENGINEERS' TOP TIP!
You don't need to use expensive or new materials for building your den. Half the fun of den building is using stuff you have lying around the house (but check before you take your nan's blanket off her).
- Tony and Satwinder

SAFETY TIPS

* Always have an adult nearby to make sure you are working safely.

  * If you need to use tools or sharp knives to make your den, always ask an adult to help. Make sure you put knives away safely when you're done.

* When using a knife, always cut away from yourself and never over your lap. If passing a knife to someone else, make sure you pass it handle first.

* Always have a first-aid kit nearby.

* Don't use anything so heavy that it would hurt you if it fell from your den.

* If you're building a den outside, find a clear, dry space. Make sure there are no dead branches above that could fall and hurt you, and never take living branches off a tree.

* Be respectful of wildlife.

* Never leave rubbish outside.

* When using spray paint, find an open, well-ventilated outdoor space.

  * Always put all tools and building materials away after use.

DENGINEERS' TOP TIP!

Get an adult to help you check that your den is safe before you play in it. Make sure nothing is moving that shouldn't be - you don't want a wobbly den.
- Sege

Materials and spaces

There are loads of different types of dens you can build, ranging from simple and temporary to more complex and permanent. Choose the one that suits you, your theme and your space best!

INDOOR COSY DEN

You'll need:
- blankets and sheets
- chairs (or sofas or even hooks on the wall to hang the blankets and sheets!)
- clothes pegs

Turn the chairs outwards. Drape blankets and sheets over the backs of the chairs so they make a roof. Use clothes pegs to secure the blankets and sheets to the chairs. Pile cushions on the floor for comfort.

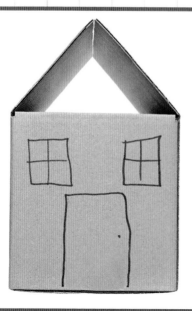

CARDBOARD CAVE

You'll need:
- cardboard boxes
- cushions and blankets
- brown paper craft tape
- paints and markers for decorating

This indoor or outdoor den can be as simple as filling a cardboard box with cushions and blankets. Or, you could use smaller boxes as bricks to build up a den shape. Or, make a more permanent structure by taping cardboard into a playhouse (see page 16). You can then have fun painting and decorating your blank canvas!

OUTDOOR TEEPEE

You'll need:
- long sticks (about 2 metres long)
- twigs, leaves, branches
- rope, string
- an adult to help!

Lay your long sticks in a bundle on the ground, ends lined up. Tie one end of the bundle together with rope. Ask an adult to help you stand the sticks upright with the rope at the top. Together, spread out the sticks into a teepee shape. Push the bottom ends into the ground. Add twigs, leaves and other branches to fill in the gaps of your den, weaving them in and securing them with string, if necessary.

OUTDOOR TREE HOUSE

You'll need:
- wood
- nails
- tools
- an adult to help!

If you have an available healthy tree and a willing adult builder, you could build a tree house den. Just be sure that it's safe!

OTHER SPACES

Look out for other spaces around you that you could turn into a den, such as:
- a window seat: surround it with blankets and sheets
- a fitted wardrobe: fill it with cushions and decorations
- a pop-up tent: use this inside or outside!
- an unused shed, spare room or garage: ask an adult if they can help you transform any of these into your own space
- tree roots: instead of building up in the trees, make yourself a shelter amongst a tree's large roots

Basic dens to build

Here are two good basic dens to start with. Once you've mastered these, you can adapt them to suit you and your theme!

CARDBOARD BOX DEN

Make yourself a private playhouse hideaway to use inside or outside. Choose a theme and decorate your den to match! To build this den, grab the biggest cardboard box you can find, another large cardboard box and some brown craft tape.

1

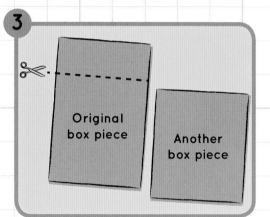

Tape the bottom of the largest box shut and leave the top flaps open. Turn the box on its long side, with the open flaps facing you.

2

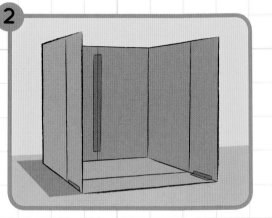

Cut off the top of the box, including the flap, as shown. Save this piece. Tape the remaining box flaps together along each bottom corner.

3

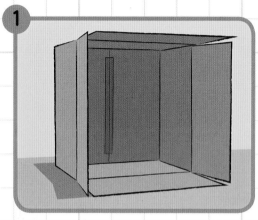

Original box piece

Another box piece

Cut off about a quarter of the short edge of the piece of cardboard you saved. Using another box folded flat, trace and cut a piece of cardboard the same size as this one.

4

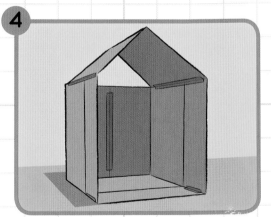

Tape the two flat pieces of cardboard together at their short edges. Then tape each outer short edge to either side of the top of the original cardboard box to make a roof. Decorate with paint and accessories!

CANOPY SHEET DEN

This den can be put up quite quickly and works in many different spaces. Find a washing line or some string, large sheets or blankets and clothes pegs. Build in your garden or in your lounge – just make sure you get permission first!

1

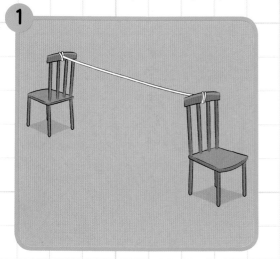

Tie a long string between two trees outside, two hooks or chairs inside, or use an existing washing line in the garden.

2

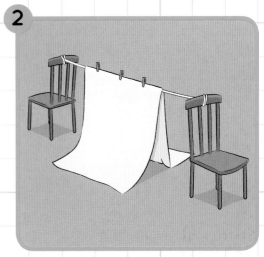

Drape your largest sheet or blanket over the string. Use clothes pegs to secure the centre of the sheet or blanket to the string or washing line.

3

Pull the bottom of the sheet outwards to make a tent shape, one side at a time. If you're building outdoors, push small sticks into the ground at each corner. Use clothes pegs to attach the corners of the fabric to the sticks. If you're building indoors, tape down the fabric corners or weigh them down with heavy books.

4

Layer more sheets and blankets over the first one if you like, for extra privacy and a cool look. Fasten these in place with clothes pegs. Then decorate inside and outside your den with fairy lights, cushions and anything else that suits your theme!

Making plans

All good buildings start with a plan. Architects sketch out diagrams to show shape, features and important materials needed. The Dengineers do the same for their dream den designs. Make your own plans in the sketching pages at the back of this book!

TOOLS

Use a pencil and some paper to get started. Grid paper is useful for following straight lines, but plain paper works too. Don't worry if your sketch isn't perfect. It's there as a guide for your build.

FLAT OR 3D?

Most floor plans are flat sketches on paper, to represent the layout of the building being designed. You could also draw your image in 3D if you want to better show how it will look.

SPECIAL FEATURES

Label any special features that you want to include in your den.

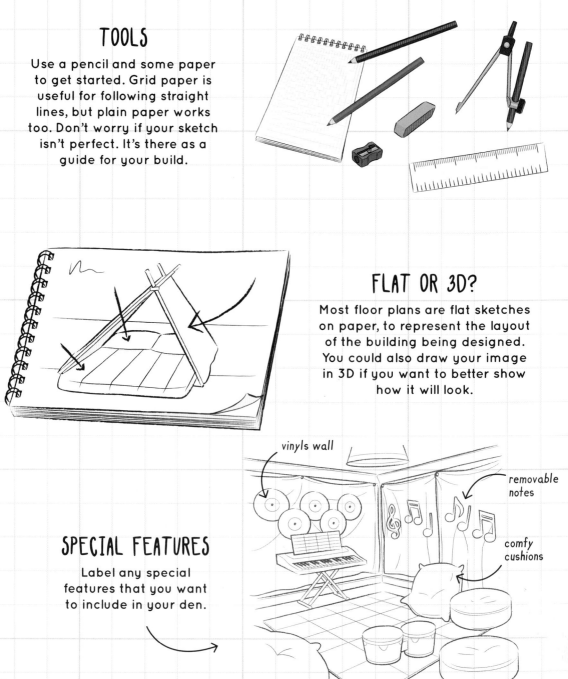

vinyls wall

removable notes

comfy cushions

SHAPE

Plan your den's shape. Is it a cardboard box playhouse, or perhaps a tent-shaped hideaway?

MATERIALS

Mark on your plans any specific materials you might need. This could include blankets, chairs, tree branches... or even plastic crates!

DENGINEERS' TOP TIP!

Every den needs to stand up. Whatever materials you choose, make sure the walls of your den will be strong enough to support themselves and the roof. Even if your roof is an old sheet, you still don't want it to fall down. - Maral

INTERIOR DETAILS

Your plan could also include a sketch of the inside of your den. Think about the little details you want to include to get your theme just right!

Making mood boards

A mood board is where you download all the ideas that are in your head on to paper or a screen. This gives you an overall vision of the style you want for your den at one quick glance.

PAPER OR SCREEN?

Cut pictures out of magazines and glue them onto A4 or poster paper for a physical collage. Or, go digital and save inspiring images from websites on to a page on-screen.

COLOUR SCHEME

By looking at your mood board, anyone should be able to tell the overall colours you're going for.

SPECTACULAR
MOVIE NIGHT!
FREE POP CORN

AT YOUR LOCAL CINEMA · FRIDAY 17:00

DENGINEERS' TOP TIP!

Choose a colour scheme rather than just your favourite colour. Pick colours that work well together and give you the mood you want in your den.
- Maral

ANYTHING GOES!

The images don't have to be things that will actually go in your den. They should just be pictures that you like - design ideas, colours, even animals - to get across the overall feel of the den.

DENGINEERS' TOP TIP!

Look for inspiration in buildings around you and take photos for your mood board. Does your local library have an interesting roof? Maybe the independent cinema has a cool exterior design? Keep an eye out! - Maral

SHORT AND SWEET
Your mood board should be a single page of the best pics that sum up your ideas.

DEN THEMES

Your dream den is all about you. Choose a theme for your personal space. What are you passionate about? Why do you need a special space? Is it a place to escape or a space to share with friends? Make sure every little detail fits with your chosen theme to create the most perfect dream den for you. Check out the 16 themes in this section for ideas, or use them as inspiration to come up with your own dream den style!

DO YOU NEED A SPACE TO...

☐ Make some noise without complaints?

☐ Craft and create in peace?

☐ Dance like no one's watching?

☐ Plan secret missions?

☐ Get together with friends?

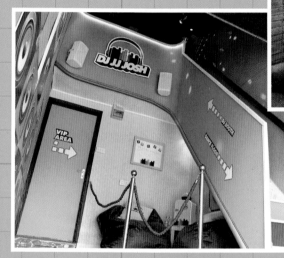

Take your theme to the extreme! Transform both the inside and outside of your den in your chosen style.

Magic or music? Sport or sewing? Find the theme that's just right for you!

Make even the smallest of spaces look totally awesome! The little details can all add up to mega wow factor.

23

SPORTS DEN

GO FOR GOLD!

Superstar athletes need a place to train, but also somewhere to plan and relax. That's where this den comes in! Whichever sport is your passion, build a gold-medal den to help you reach your athletic goals.

WHERE TO BUILD?

Think about how you want to use the den. Is it a place to practise and train? If so, you might want a permanent space for your equipment, and easy access to the garden too. Ask an adult to help you transform a shed or garage. If the den is instead going to be for watching matches, planning tactics and chilling after a day of sports out on the field, you could build a cosy blanket tent in your bedroom or a cardboard cave in the lounge.

INSPIRATION!

The Dengineers designers have built loads of sport-themed dens on the programme. See which of their ideas you could bring into your den at home!

MULTI SPORTS

This den was a true sports fanatic's dream. Shaped like a sports stadium, it had a tyre podium outside and exercise mats inside for training to become the best all-round athlete ever.

Paint a running track on the wall of your den for a competitive look.

RUGBY

The Dengineers' rugby den was shaped like a rugby ball, creating a snug space inside for watching matches with mates.

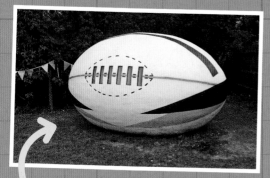

Plan your team's tactics! Find a magnetic whiteboard from an office supply or bargain shop. Draw the pitch with whiteboard markers. Then use coloured magnets to mark out players and plays.

What team do you support? Use their colours as your den's colour scheme.

FOOTBALL

Passion for a favourite team was the theme for this football den. It was based on the team's colours and stadium.

Watch the game in peace! Build your den around the telly, or bring a tablet into a pop-up den for private viewing.

MARTIAL ARTS

The outside of this den was based on a traditional Japanese teahouse, while the inside took inspiration from a dojo training hall.

Ask an adult to help you put up equipment like a punch bag and chin-up bar for serious skills sessions.

CRICKET

This build brought the cricket ground home with a covered den in the garden, perfect for practising skills in all weathers.

Ask an adult to help you attach old cricket bats to the wall of your den. If you position them flat, they can become shelves for balls!

CYCLING

It was pedal to the medal with this helmet-shaped cycling den. Bikes could even be secured inside for training!

Paint or print out pictures of cheering fans. Stick these to your den's walls for inspiration as you train. Go you!

UPCYCLE PROJECT! TEAM SHIRT CUSHIONS

Cool down with these properly pro cushions. You'll need old team shirts (find these around your house or at charity shops), a needle and thread and some cotton filling.

1

Sew each sleeve of the shirt shut. Sew the bottom edges together, too.

2

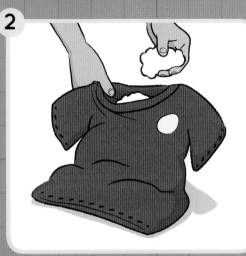

Push stuffing through the neck hole until the shirt is full of cotton filling. Make sure you get it all the way down to the bottom and in the sleeves too.

3

Sew the neck hole shut to complete your cushion.

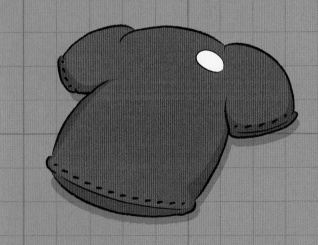

Place your comfy team cushion in your den!

MAGIC DEN

ROLL UP, ROLL UP!

Whether you're into classic tricks, sleight of hand or witchcraft and wizardry, make your dream magic den appear with these ideas from the programme.

WHERE TO BUILD?

Magicians never reveal their tricks! Find yourself a private place to practise your craft in peace until it's perfect. You might want to add in an area to perform your magic show, too. Try transforming your fitted wardrobe into a secret planning space, building a magical blanket den under a table or even pitching a mystical pop-up tent.

DENGINEERS' TOP TIP!

Magic is full of surprises, so make sure your den has some unexpected elements. Maybe it could have a secret entrance, a false wall or a hidden box for all your tricks.
- Emma

GOING CLASSIC

The Dengineers designers delved into their box of tricks to create this traditional yet modern magic dream den, full of cards, illusions and classic colours. Try these ideas for your own magic den, if classic magic is your thing.

BLACK, WHITE AND RED

Take colour inspiration from the magician's all-important piece of equipment: a pack of playing cards.

INSPIRATION!

SHOWTIME

Make yourself a space to perform your show. This could be a cleared area in front of your den or a large piece of cardboard laid down flat. Paint the cardboard in a black and white grid pattern for a theatrical effect.

SECRET SPACE

Put up a blanket or cardboard screen to create a space behind your stage where you can prepare your tricks in private.

FLOATING CARDS

Ask an adult to help pierce a small hole in the top of playing cards with a needle. Thread clear fishing line through each hole and tie this to the ceiling to create the illusion that each card is floating in the air.

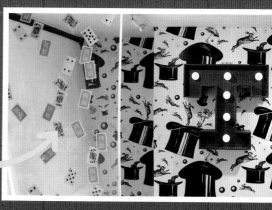

29

WITCHCRAFT AND WIZARDRY

If witchcraft and wizardry are more up your sleeve, conjure up
a fantasy magic den fit for the finest of witches and wizards.

DEN SORCERY

This den on the programme was
based around a wizard's hat.
The Dengineers gave it a dusty,
crooked feel, and broomsticks
were in prime place. Have you
got a broomstick of your own?
If so, put it on display!

INSPIRATION!

FANTASTICAL DETAILS

Decorate your den with all things mystical:
potions, magic wands, witch or wizard hats...
even owl figures!

SPELL IT OUT

Place a chair or comfy floor
cushions inside your den for your
own spot to sit and come up with
spells. Don't forget a spell book
and pen too!

UPCYCLE PROJECT!
COMFY CAULDRON

Do you have a small dog or cat who would like to hang out in your den? Transform an old cooking pot into a comfy cauldron bed just for them! Ask for permission to use a large pot from home that is no longer needed, or find one at a charity shop. You'll also need sandpaper, gold paint and a small cushion.

1

Use sandpaper to sand down the outside of the cooking pot, including the lid. Paint the pot and lid black, if they aren't already. Leave to dry.

2

Paint the rim of the lid gold. Then use the gold paint to decorate the pot. You could paint your dog or cat's initial on the front, or go for a magical starry pattern all the way around. Leave your decorations to dry.

3

Place a small cushion at the bottom of the pot to keep your pet comfy. Then put your cool cauldron inside your den!

If you don't have a pet, this upcycled cauldron is also perfect for storage in your den. Use it for magic books, wands or anything else you can think of!

CODING DEN

DENS GO DIGITAL!

Create your very own coding cave – the perfect place to indulge your passion for all things maths, coding and computers. Give your den a digital, electronic vibe, then give yourself a high-tech high-five!

WHERE TO BUILD?

This den can be as simple or as complex as you like. You could create a cosy cave from cardboard or sheets in a quiet spot in your house. Then bring a laptop inside for low-key coding. Or, clear a section of your bedroom or a spare room (if you have permission) and add gadgets and tech for a more permanent themed space.

PIXEL PATTERN

Cut squares from different coloured paper, using the colour scheme you've chosen for your den. Then stick these on the wall of your den to create a cool pixel pattern.

INSPIRATION!

DESK SPACE

This den is serious stuff! Turn an existing desk into your coding space and build your den around it. Or, ask an adult to help you mount a flat piece of wood on the wall for an ultra-modern floating workspace.

GAMING CHAIR

If you have space in your den, you could bring in a gaming chair to feel the part of a coding king or queen.

DENGINEERS' TOP TIP!

Do you need light and power for your den? Think about how you will get that to your den location.
- Tony and Satwinder

WHAT IS CODING?

Coding is writing instructions for a computer to follow. It can be used to make machines work, tell robots what to do, create video game worlds and so much more.

PUT YOURSELF IN THE GAME...

Try adding these digital details to your den at home.

HIGH TECH

Bring your coding equipment into your den, such as a laptop, tablet or phone – if your friendly adult will lend you theirs.

LOW TECH

Go retro with a low-tech notebook and pens for your maths notes and workings-out.

PROGRAMMABLE PIECES

If you have a permanent space and a bit of money to spend, you could have fun finding programmable pieces at computer shops or online. The Dengineers added these programmable lights and this codable wall-climbing robot to the den on the programme for hands-on coding practice.

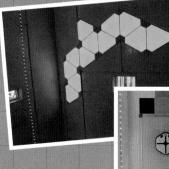

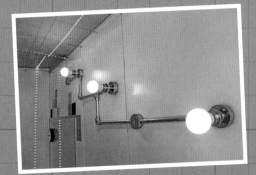

LIGHTING

Create a futuristic feel with various types of lighting. This den used both strip lights and spotlights for a cool computer look. Find battery-powered lights that you can place on the floor or walls of your den.

UPCYCLE PROJECT! TECHIE WALL ART

Make art for your den out of bits of old tech. Ask an adult for unused circuit boards, cables, keyboards and whatever else they can find. These are hard to recycle, so they're perfect to reuse! Just be sure they are disconnected and safe. You'll also need a large sheet of cardboard or wood for the background.

1

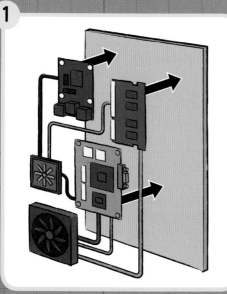

On the cardboard or wood, lay out the pieces of old tech in the pattern you'd like for your art. Then glue each piece in place, one at a time.

2

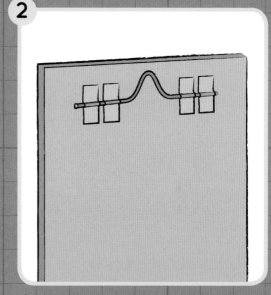

On the back of the cardboard or wood, glue or tape a piece of wire to create a hanging loop, as shown. When this is dry, ask an adult to help you hang your art on the wall with a nail and hammer.

NOTE: If you don't want to put a hole in the wall, use a sticky wall hanger, or just prop up your art in your den. But be careful – the tech will make it heavy!

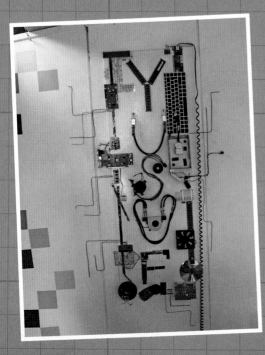

ROYAL DEN

ROYAL SEAL OF APPROVAL!

Live like a king or queen in your very own royal den. Take inspiration from the palaces and monarchs of the past to make a palatial hideaway where you can lounge in luxury.

WHERE TO BUILD?

A regal den should be one of epic proportions. How about transforming your entire bedroom into a grand castle? Turn the inside of the bedroom into a drawing room with plenty of royal details (see the next page for ideas). For the entrance to your fine fortress, ask an adult to help you make a cardboard castle wall – complete with drawbridge – to place in front of your bedroom door. Only those deemed worthy by the king or queen shall pass!

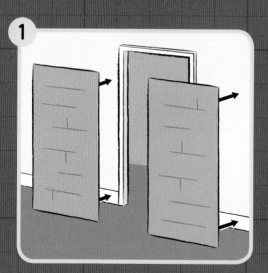

1

Piece and tape together some cardboard to make two large rectangles, each the size of your bedroom door. Place one rectangle on either side of the door, just slightly overlapping the doorway, as shown. Ask an adult to help you attach the rectangles to the wall using strong tape or nails.

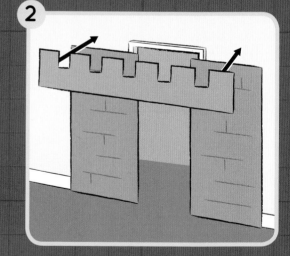

2

Piece and tape together more cardboard into a thick strip long enough to go across the top of both rectangles. Cut evenly spaced squares down into the strip to create the battlements across the top, as shown. Attach this strip to the wall as in step 1.

3

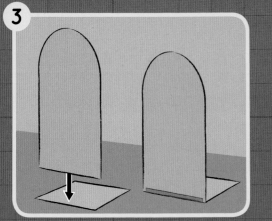

For the drawbridge, piece and tape together cardboard to create an arched rectangle shape to fit your doorway. Then cut out a large square piece of cardboard, each side the length of the bottom edge of your drawbridge. Tape one edge of the square to the bottom of the drawbridge to create a hinge.

4

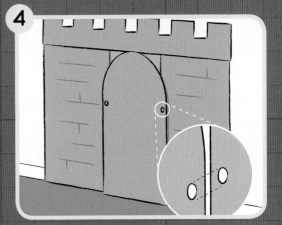

Stand the drawbridge in your doorway and tape the large square on the floor so the drawbridge won't slide. Ask an adult to use a large needle to poke a hole on each side of the drawbridge, near the top. Poke holes directly behind these in the cardboard rectangles overlapping the doorway.

5

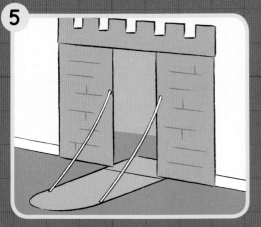

Thread string through one cardboard wall hole, towards the bedroom. Tie the end in a knot big enough that it can't fit through the hole. Let the drawbridge lie flat on the floor. Thread the string through the corresponding hole in the drawbridge. Tie a large knot on the outside of the drawbridge to hold the string in place, then cut off the excess. Repeat for the holes on the other side.

6

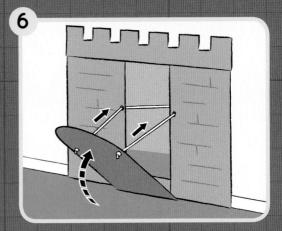

To pull up your drawbridge, stand inside your bedroom and pull on the knots behind the cardboard walls.

INSPIRATION!

FIRST IMPRESSIONS...

Decorate the outside of your den in royal style with these ideas from *The Dengineers*.

STONE EFFECT

Before taping your cardboard castle in place, you could paint it to look like stone. Paint the cardboard light brown or grey as a base colour. Paint dark brown or grey lines to make brick shapes, then use a sponge to dab on grey paint all over.

INSPIRATION!

PILLARS AND TURRETS

Go even grander with fancy columns or turrets. Curve large pieces of cardboard and ask an adult to help you stick these to your castle walls with strong tape. Paint vertical lines down each one.

CUSTOM COAT OF ARMS

Royal families have their own coats of arms: a shield with a design special to the family. Design and cut out your own to put up on your den's doorway. Think about using your initials and pictures of objects that show your interests.

FLY THE FLAG

Make a flag for your castle. Print out a picture from the Internet or draw your own. This could be the flag of your favourite country, your initials or an image that represents you. Tape it to a stick or dowel for your den.

INNER DETAILS...

For a grand interior fit for a king or queen, try adding your own version of these regal *Dengineers* touches.

CROWN JEWELS

Do you have a collection of royal items? Display them on shelves in your room. Make yourself a crown to display too, to remind everyone of your royal status! Cut a strip of card large enough to fit around your head. Cut an ornamental pattern into the top of the card, then paint the card gold. Glue on gems for added glitz. Ask an adult to help you wrap the card around your head and tape the ends together.

DENGINEERS' TOP TIP!

To create a royal look, think carefully about colour. Whatever colour you choose, make sure it's a strong one. For example, a touch of gold can turn any chair into a throne.
- Emma

SUMPTUOUS SEATING

Rest your royal bottom on something special. This could be your very own throne, or a luxurious chaise longue. For a throne, ask an adult to help you find an old chair at home or at a charity shop. Paint it gold and decorate it with royal touches, such as fabric sashes. Or, see if you can find a chaise longue at a charity shop and add a cushion for comfort.

CRAFT DEN

SEW GOOD!

Escape to a world of creativity in your very own craft den. Whether you're creating just for fun or you dream of becoming a famous artist or designer, make yourself a special space to let your imagination run free.

WHERE TO BUILD?

The ideal craft den would have a crafting table and loads of storage for supplies. If you have space for these two things, that's the space for your den! A section of your room or a spare room would do nicely, or ask an adult to help you fix up an unused shed, if possible. If space is limited, instead make yourself a blanket or cardboard den that can become an inspirational space to craft in. Just bring your supplies in, and get crafting!

PATCHWORK PERFECT

Give your crafting den a true homemade feel with a patchwork floor. Cut equal-sized squares from different coloured pieces of card. Tape these together at the edges, then lay the large patchwork piece over your den's floor. If you're a sewing whizz, you could sew together squares of fabric instead of paper to make a patchwork blanket to lay down on the ground.

CUTE AS A BUTTON

Decorate your den with giant buttons like *The Dengineers* designers did. For your version, cut large circles out of coloured card. Draw four black dots on each circle to make the buttonholes. Stick the buttons on your den's walls using sticky tack (or safety pins if your den is made of sheets and blankets).

INSPIRATION!

Make It Easy

Sew, Sew Happy

Stitch In Time

DESIGNER'S DESK

If you've got space, give yourself a crafting table in your den. You could build the den around an existing desk, or ask an adult to help you bring one in. If you're using a blanket or cardboard den, just clear a working space on the floor and protect it with newspaper or plastic sheets. You could even buy a mini ironing board that you could bring in for a crafting table on the go. Just fold it away when you're done!

WIND THE BOBBIN UP...

Try out these CRAFTY ways to store your bits and bobs.

JOLLY JARS

Use all sorts of clear jars and containers for clever, colourful storage solutions. Find these around your house (such as clean empty jam jars) or buy them at craft or discount shops. Fill each one with a different craft supply.

MULTIPURPOSE MUGS

For long items that won't fit inside a closed jar, get creative with other types of storage that you can find around your house. Patterned mugs are perfect for holding supplies like paintbrushes or knitting needles – and they look sweet too!

HANDY HANGERS

Save trouser hangers that have an opening at one end. Slide rolls of ribbon or tape on to the straight piece for easy access. Then hang the hangers around your den!

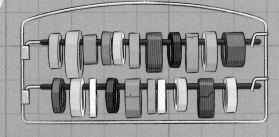

DENGINEERS' TOP TIP!

Make sure you have lots of storage for all your supplies. Different shaped containers add a bit of interest to your den. How about putting buttons in a jar or ribbon on hangers?
- Emma

MAKE A GIANT BOBBIN

1

Starting at the bottom of a cardboard tube, carefully wind wool or string around it, gluing it in place as you go. Continue until you reach the top. Snip and glue the end of the wool or string in place.

2

Cut two circles out of card, making them slightly larger than the ends of the tube. Glue these to each end of the reel.

DENGINEERING ENGINEERING

Did you know that a piece of wool has the same structure as wire cables that are used for building work?

A single fibre of string or wire isn't very strong.

When fibres are wound round together, forming wool or cable strands, they gain much more strength.

Thin wire cables made of many strands are strong enough to work in lifts and cranes!

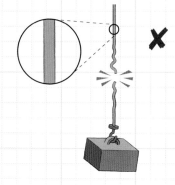

DANCE DEN

FEEL THE BEAT!

Dance all day in your very own ultimate dance studio den. Find yourself a dream den space for perfecting your moves and performing for your adoring fans.

WHERE TO BUILD?

This den should be tall enough for you to stand – and dance – in! You'll need somewhere with a bit of space to create a dance floor, too. If you can clear a section of your bedroom or a spare room, that would be best. Or, ask an adult to help you convert an unused garage or cellar. If you don't have space for a permanent dance den, don't worry! Start with a cosy blanket or cardboard box den (see page 14) where you can curl up and watch dance videos to study your favourite moves.

ZING!

Use loads of bright colours to decorate your dance den. This creates an upbeat and inspirational space.

INSPIRATION!

CHILL-OUT ZONE

You'll need somewhere to recharge after all that dancing! Bring big cushions or beanbag chairs into your den for chill-out breaks.

BALLET BARRE

Ask an adult to help you mount a ballet barre on your den's wall. You can find these at specialist fitness shops, or you could use a sturdy curtain rod.

INSPIRATION!

MIRRORS

Ask an adult to help you attach some mirrors to your den's walls. Find full-length mirrors or smaller framed ones - anything that helps you see yourself dance! If you have a wardrobe in the room, stick mirrors to its outer door. Or, even better, build your den around an existing mirrored wardrobe!

DANCE FLOOR

Make sure to clear floor space big enough for dance practice in your den! Use this for rehearsals and performances too.

SPARKLE LIKE A TRUE DANCE STAR...

Add dazzling details to your own dance den.

DISCO DAZZLE

Ask an adult to help you hang a glitter ball from the ceiling for that all-important dance party feel.

BLAST THE BEATS

Bring in portable speakers and a TV, laptop, tablet or phone – if your friendly adult will lend you theirs – to watch dance videos and blast your music for dance practice.

SPOTLIGHT ON YOU

Find battery-powered lights at DIY shops to place around the room as spotlights. Leave them on the floor to light up your stage, or ask an adult to help you mount them high on the wall to shine down on you.

BOLLYWOOD BLING...

If you're inspired by the music and moves of Indian Bollywood films, give your dance den a Bollywood bling theme!

STAR OF THE SHOW

Print pictures of yourself dancing. Stick these on the walls for inspiration.

LOUNGING IN LUXURY

Drape curtains or sheets on the wall for a rich feel.

INSPIRATION!

RICH REDS

Give your den a regal feel with a rich colour palette of reds, maroons and golds.

BLING FOR A BOLLYWOOD KING OR QUEEN

Instead of beanbag chairs, adorn a larger chair with sequins and gold decorations to look like your throne. Place silky cushions on the floor, too.

LAVISH LANTERNS

Make your own mood lighting for your den using clean empty jars, acrylic paint and craft jewels.

1. Paint intricate patterns on the jars using gold acrylic paint. Leave to dry.

2. Ask an adult to help you use a glue gun to glue jewels in place. Leave to dry.

3. Place a battery-powered light inside each lantern (not candles!).

MUSIC DEN

MAKE SOME NOISE!

If you are a budding superstar DJ or rockin' musician, then this is the den theme for you! Give your family some peace and quiet, and create an inspiring musical space for yourself, where you can be as loud as you want.

WHERE TO BUILD?

This den is best suited to a room that can be soundproofed so that you can rock out to your heart's content – without complaints from family or friends! See if you can get permission to transform an unused shed, spare bedroom or garage.

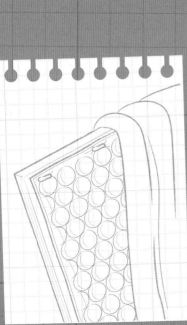

⚒ DENGINEERING ENGINEERING

Sound is vibration. To soundproof something, you need to stop the vibration from getting through. That usually means packing walls full of materials so tightly that they can't vibrate. They'll then absorb the sound instead of letting it pass through. For your home den, layer insulation over your walls, such as foam or bubble wrap covered with blankets. Ask an adult to help you stick them up with a staple gun or string.

DANCE FLOOR

On the programme, the Dengineers created this DJ lounge. Try some of their ideas to create your own version of a DJ den at home. Make sure you include dancing space for epic parties in your own DJ den!

VIP AREA

Give VIPs (you and your mates!) a special spot to chill. Fill it with beanbag chairs or comfy cushions, stock it with snacks and use ropes to keep non-VIPs out.

CENTRE STAGE

The Dengineers also created a rock music den. Try a rock theme in your home den, complete with a stage space and rock logo. Ask an adult to help you build a stage out of plywood, or simply use flat cardboard to turn your den into the coolest gig venue around.

SUPERSTAR IN THE MAKING...

Try these ideas for your own music den.

CREATE YOUR OWN LOGO

Design a logo for your DJ
or band name. Paint several
copies, cut them out and stick
them all over your den to get
your brand out there!

COMPOSE A MASTERPIECE

Paint a music stave on poster paper and
stick it on the wall. Draw some clefs and
notes, or print images from the Internet. Cut
these out and put sticky tack on the back
of each one. Stick them on the stave and
shuffle them around to compose on the go.

BRING IN THE KIT!

If you've got musical
instruments or DJ kit, bring
them in to your den and
make some noise!

DENGINEERS' TOP TIP!

It's easy to turn everyday objects into musical instruments.
Look around and have fun making and decorating your own
instruments. You could make a cool rain stick by sealing
dry rice in a cardboard tube, or how about a nifty guitar
made out of a shoebox and some elastic bands?
– Emma

UPCYCLE PROJECT! WALL OF FAME

Create the coolest wall ever! Ask an adult for some unwanted old-school vinyls, or buy a stack at a charity shop. You'll also need coloured card and silver spray paint.

1

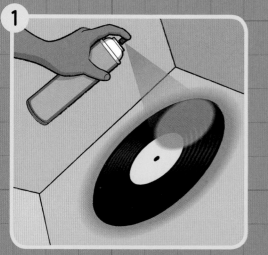

Clean the vinyls. Then place them in a cardboard box in an open outdoor space and ask an adult to help you spray paint each one silver. Leave to dry.

2

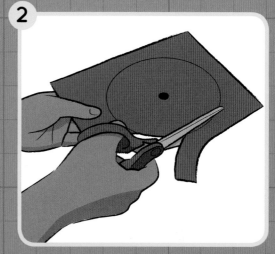

From a piece of card, cut out a circle to fit the centre of your vinyls. Trace this circle on different coloured pieces of card. Cut out enough for one for each of your vinyls. Draw a little black circle in the centre of each one.

3

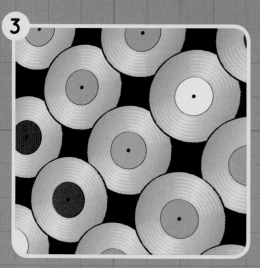

Glue a coloured circle to each of your vinyls. Then stick the vinyls up on your wall!

If you don't have old vinyls, or if you prefer a more modern look, paint or print out colourful speaker graphics instead. Put these up on the wall in a cool grid pattern. Add sound lines for added effect.

51

CINEMA DEN

LIGHTS, CAMERA
ACTION!

Step back in time to the days of Hollywood glamour. Build yourself a cinema-themed den for some serious film viewing, or use it as an inspirational space to create your own movie masterpieces!

WHERE TO BUILD?

The perfect cinema den is somewhere you can dim the lights. Build a cosy space in front your telly by hanging up sheets and blankets. (Don't drape anything over your TV.) Or, if you have a portable laptop, tablet or projector, find a dark space, such as under the table or stairs, or even in a pop-up tent. Lay down cushions on the floor for comfy viewing with friends.

INSPIRATION!

BOX OFFICE
Find a cardboard box big enough for you to sit
inside. Ask an adult to help you cut window flaps
out of one side. Make a retro BOX OFFICE sign
and glue it above the flap on the outside of
the box. Ask friends and family for their tickets
when they arrive for your next movie night!

RETRO SIGNS
Draw black blocky letters on
white poster paper to make
signs for your cinema.

FILM POSTERS
Cut images from
magazines, print
pictures from the
Internet or take your
own photos to give
yourself a starring
role! Stick these up as
fun film posters inside
and outside your den.

RED CARPET
Lay down a red blanket or sheet to create a fabulous
entrance to your den, ready for the grand premiere.

BEHIND THE SCENES....

Try adding these touches to your own cinema den.

HOLLYWOOD STARS

Cut large star shapes out of card. Paint them with gold paint and leave to dry. Then lay the stars on your den floor for some Hollywood glitz and glam!

DIRECTOR'S CUT

Roll a piece of black card into a cone shape, leaving a small opening at the pointy end. Tape along the long edge. Write or stencil 'DIRECTOR' on the outside. Cut a strip of card and tape each end on to the cone to make a handle. Then shout out your director's orders through your megaphone!

TAKE 1!

Make a clapperboard for a cool prop in your den – or for calling the shots! Start with black card, or paint a piece of card black. From another piece of black card, cut a thin strip the length of the long edge of the first piece, leaving a notch poking down at one end. Use a split pin to connect the notch on the strip to the top left corner of the larger card. Write your film's details on the board using white paint and a fine brush.

MAKE AN AWARDS STATUE

1

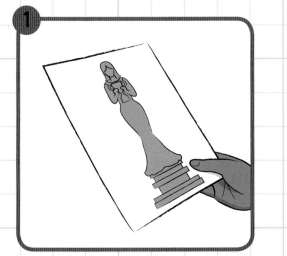

Draw a basic human shape on a piece of A4 card. Draw a base connected to it, as shown. Paint the whole shape gold, or decorate it to look like you! Cut it out. Repeat this so you have two identical cut-out figures.

2

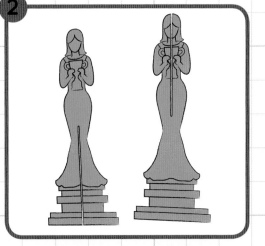

In the centre of the first shape, cut a line from the bottom up to the halfway point. In the centre of the second shape, cut a line from the top down to the halfway point.

3

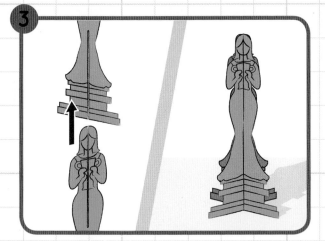

Slot the two pieces together. Then display your award in your den, or present it to a winning friend!

On the programme, the Dengineers made this award using 3D printing!

LIBRARY DEN

SHHHHH!

Do you need a quiet place to read? Or write? Or both? Then it's time to build a library den! Give your den a magical feel and escape into the world of books.

WHERE TO BUILD?

Your library den needs to be a cosy escape. Do you have a fitted wardrobe big enough to fill with books and cushions? Or a window seat that you can surround with blankets and sheets? Or, try building your own structure that you can put in a quiet place (see pages 16 and 17). This den is best kept inside to keep your books dry, unless you have a waterproof shed you can use.

DENGINEERS' TOP TIP!

Use lighting to create a comfy reading area, but be careful not to make it too bright. You want your library to have a relaxed feel. – Maral

NOTICEBOARD
Put up a cork noticeboard for a library feel.

FAIRY LIGHTS
Add a little magic and a gentle glow with a string of delicate fairy lights.

BOOKS, BOOKS, BOOKS!
Pack every nook and cranny with books to read and notebooks to fill.

COSY SEATS
A beanbag or rolled-up blankets are perfect for curling up with a good book.

DON'T JUDGE A DEN BY ITS COVER (OR DO!)...

Think about these ideas for the outside of your own library den.

ENCHANTED FOREST

Ask an adult to help you cut large tree and branch shapes out of cardboard or wood. Paint them brown to look like tree bark. Secure these to the outside of your den for a magical, mystical woodland feel. Then, when you're writing in your den, look out through the trees for inspiration!

INSPIRATION!

FAIRY GARDEN

Help your imagination blossom with a bewitching fairy garden. If your den is indoors, use potted or artificial plants. Find or make little fairy dolls to hide in the garden, too!

UPCYCLE PROJECT!
SECRET STORAGE BOOKS

Ask an adult for an unwanted book ready for a new life. This could be one you have at home or a charity shop find.

1

Open the book to a few pages in. Paint PVA glue on the three outer edges of the book to stick the pages together, leaving the open pages loose. Leave to dry.

2

2 cm

Using a ruler and pencil, mark a rectangle on the top page of your glued book block. This should be about 2 cm in from each edge.

3

Ask an adult to help you cut out the rectangle with a craft knife, several pages at a time. Leave a few pages at the bottom of the book block. Then glue along the cut edges of the rectangle. Leave to dry.

Now hide your best pens or notes with your top-secret story ideas inside!

SPY DEN

TOP SECRET!

Mastermind your missions in an ultra-cool, top-secret spy-themed den. Fill it with super-sleuth gadgets, hidden compartments and your own secret agent look.

WHERE TO BUILD?

This den is all about secrecy. You want the outside of your den to look completely normal. It shouldn't look like a den at all! Then on the inside, it can open into your own secret spy space. A cleared-out fitted wardrobe in a bedroom is perfect for this. Prepare to lead your double life!

This looks like an ordinary wardrobe in a completely normal bedroom...

But slide the door and there's a spy den hidden inside!

DENGINEERS' TOP TIP!

Camouflage is key! Think about how your den can be hidden from friends and family.
- Tony and Satwinder

DISGUISES

A good spy is always prepared for any mission. Be ready to go undercover with a selection of wigs, hats and whatever other costumes you can gather together.

HIDEAWAY HOLES

Collect foam sheets from packaging. Place an object you want to hide against the foam. Ask an adult to help you cut carefully and snugly around the object. Remove the foam piece. Then tuck the object inside, hidden away!

61

HOW TO BECOME A SPY...

Bring these ideas into your own spy den.

SECRET AGENT CODE NAME

A spy never reveals their own name. Come up with an alias for your double life as a spy. This is normally a first name and a surname, such as Lucy Leopard. You could choose names that you like, or open a book, close your eyes and point to words for a more random approach.

SECRET AGENT LOGO

Design a logo that represents your alias. Think of colours and shapes that mean something to you. Use this logo to decorate your den!

SECRET AGENT CODE

It is incredibly important that messages between spies can't be understood by anyone else. Come up with your own code that you can use between you and your agent friends. You need to associate a new letter or symbol with each letter of the alphabet.

The reverse alphabet code is a good starting point:

A	B	C	D	E	F	G	H	I	J	K	L	M	N	O	P	Q	R	S	T	U	V	W	X	Y	Z
Z	Y	X	W	V	U	T	S	R	Q	P	O	N	M	L	K	J	I	H	G	F	E	D	C	B	A

Write out your message using the coded letters. For example:

XLNV GL NB WVM means COME TO MY DEN!

Think about how things in your den can have a double life of their own. For example, this picture on the wall actually pulls down to become a desk and holder for hidden spy notes and files. Make your own version with a piece of cardboard folded in half. Decorate the outside as an innocent picture. Then fold it up and tuck top-secret spy papers inside!

INVISIBLE INK

Use invisible ink to write messages to your agent friends. No one will even know the words are there!

1

Squeeze the juice of one lemon into a bowl. Add a few drops of water. Mix together.

2

Dip a cotton bud into the mixture and use this to write your message on a piece of white paper. Leave to dry so the message disappears.

3

To read the message, ask an adult to help you heat the paper by holding it near a lightbulb. The lemon juice oxidizes (mixes with oxygen) and turns brown when heated!

TRANSPORT DEN

Whether you're into planes, trains, cars, boats or anything else that goes, make yourself a transport-themed den for a place to build and display your models. Put yourself in the driving seat!

DESTINATION: DREAM DEN!

WHERE TO BUILD?

Because you are likely to build and display your model planes, trains and more in this den, it works best as a permanent structure. Do you have space in a loft that you have permission to use? Or a spare room? Or even an empty outdoor shed? If not, build yourself a den using large cardboard boxes (see pages 14 and 16).

INSPIRATION!

BEN'S STATION

TICKET OFFICE

SIGNAL BOX

Paint a shoebox black. Cut out two circles from a piece of card. Paint one red and one green. Use sticky tack to display the green one when you're in your den and the red one when you're out!

PLATFORM

Cut thick strips of cardboard or plywood (ask an adult to help!) and lay them alongside each other to create a platform at the front of your den.

On the inside, create a cockpit or dashboard out of cardboard. Paint it black then use paint, pens, buttons and old plastic lids to create the controls. Don't forget a chair to sit in, too!

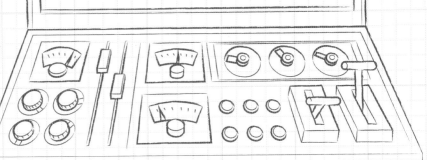

You could make the outside of your den look like the front of a vehicle. Include a small window to look through when you're in the driver's seat inside.

SIGNS

Cut out cardboard signs and paint these in vintage colours like red and green. Give your den its own station name.

DENGINEERS' TOP TIP!

Whatever type of transport is your favourite, make the driving seat the main feature of the den. Think about how you can feel in control, as if you're actually driving, flying, sailing, etc.!
- Sege

MODEL MANIA...

Travel far with more ideas from *The Dengineers* for your own den.

COMMUNICATIONS TERMINAL

Paint an old shoebox a solid colour. Decorate it with dials to make it look like an old-fashioned communications console. Store a walkie-talkie inside, and put another walkie-talkie near friends or family. This way you can keep in touch, and easily ask for snacks to be delivered when you need refuelling!

MODEL TABLE

Find a piece of plywood or an old table to use for your model building. For a clever use of space, ask an adult to help you cut a circle out of the centre, big enough for you to stand in!

FLYING HIGH

Ask an adult to help you string your finished models from the roof of your den.

DENGINEERING ENGINEERING

Ever wondered why WWII military buildings were curved and not flat-roofed? Because an arch is actually stronger! You can see this with a piece of card and some bricks. If the card is laid flat and a brick is placed in the middle, the card collapses. But when the card is arched between the bricks and the brick is set on top, it stays in place!

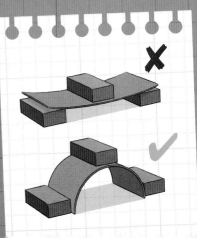

Make handy holders for all your model-building bits and bobs with old cereal boxes and wrapping paper.

1

Carefully cut the top off a cereal box as shown.

2

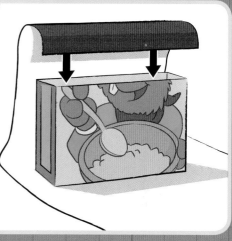

Wrap gift wrap around the box, tucking the edges inside. Glue in place.

Repeat for as many storage boxes as you like! Then fill with all your building bits for mega model organisation.

ADVENTURE DEN

GO WILD!

This is the ultimate outdoor den. Be ready for adventure, to watch wildlife and to hide away in your own secret hut.

WHERE TO BUILD?

This den is all about survival and adventure in the great outdoors, so a den outside is definitely best! Build a structure in your garden or nearby woodland, or customise an existing space, such as underneath a hedge, amongst large tree roots or even in an old shed (with permission!).

BUILD UP

A good adventurer has a full view of their surroundings. If it's safe and you have space, ask an adult to help you build your den up high so you can look out for danger... and pesky grown-ups, too.

INSPIRATION!

TREEHOUSE

The most famous way to build up is the ever-popular treehouse den. Find a healthy, strong tree and get to work. With an adult's help, you could make yourself a simple platform out of plywood resting on low branches. Or, ask an adult who is really good at DIY to build you a shed higher up in the tree out of wood and nails.

BUILD DOWN

If you're after a hideaway rather than a lookout, building a den deep down might be better for you. A den like this can be camouflaged to blend in with its surroundings – perfect for watching wildlife without being seen.

TREE BUNKER

Build a den around a fallen tree or a tree with high roots. Look for natural materials you can use, like fallen branches and vines in the woods around you. Dig down into the dirt even further for a super-secret hideout! (Ask an adult to check it's safe.)

1. Lean tall branches against a fallen tree to build your frame. Tie these together with rope or vines.

2. Fill in the gaps with more branches. Tie each one in place.

3. Weave twigs through the large branches to make your den more secure.

4. Cover your den with leaves and grass to camouflage it.

THREE THINGS TO THINK ABOUT FOR CAMOUFLAGING YOUR DEN:

1. **Shape:** Most things in nature aren't straight or sharp-angled. Use curves and gentle slopes instead.

2. **Shine:** In a woodland, not much shines. If it does, it catches the eye of wildlife and scares it away. Avoid using anything shiny on your den!

3. **Colour:** Always choose colours that match the surroundings of your den. Usually this means lovely shades of green and brown!

A DENGINEER ADVENTURER IS ALWAYS PREPARED...

Bring these survival den ideas into your own den.

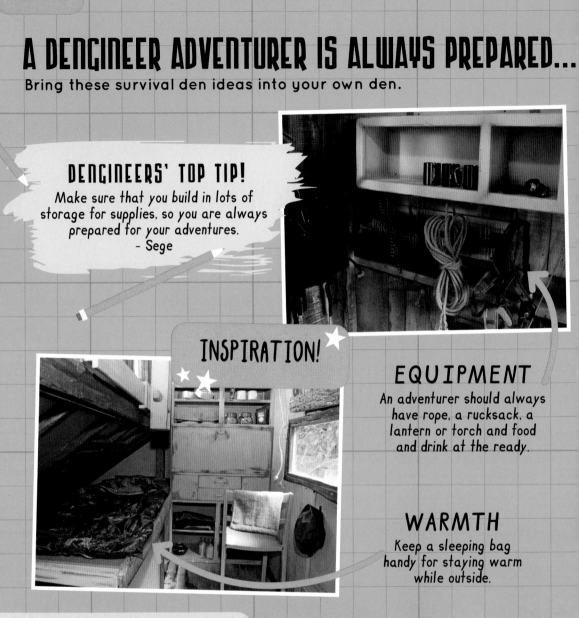

DENGINEERS' TOP TIP!

Make sure that you build in lots of storage for supplies, so you are always prepared for your adventures.
- Sege

INSPIRATION!

EQUIPMENT

An adventurer should always have rope, a rucksack, a lantern or torch and food and drink at the ready.

WARMTH

Keep a sleeping bag handy for staying warm while outside.

PULL-UP SNACK BUCKET

If you're building a den up high, you'll need an easy way to bring up supplies. That's where this pull-up snack bucket comes in! To make your own: find or make a bucket. Cut a piece of rope long enough to reach from the ground up to your den. Tie one end of the rope around the bucket's handle. Ask an adult to fill the bucket with snacks, then pull it up by the other end of the rope to your private eating place!

MAKE A PERISCOPE

A periscope is a clever way to see outside without being seen. Using two mirrors at 45° angles, you can peer through the bottom of the periscope and see what's in its line of vision at the top. Just find a shoebox, two small mirrors and a protractor to make your own version!

1

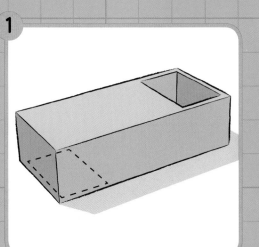

Tape the lid in place on your shoebox. Ask an adult to help you cut a rectangle across one end of the lid, as shown. Cut another rectangle across the opposite end of the bottom of the box.

2

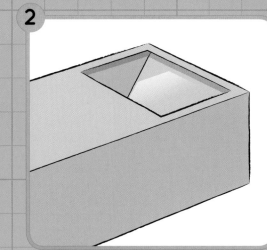

Place the first mirror inside the first rectangle with the reflective surface facing the opening. Use a protractor to position the mirror at a 45° angle from the end of thebox. Glue or tape in place.

3

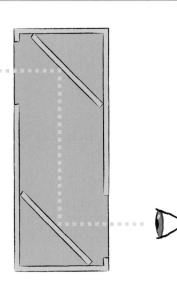

Repeat step 2 with the other mirror in the other rectangle opening.

Paint the periscope green to blend in with your camouflaged den.

ECO DEN

REDUCE, REUSE, RECYCLE!

Do your bit for the environment with an eco extravaganza of a den! Challenge yourself to use as many recycled materials as possible, and make use of the earth around you, too.

WHERE TO BUILD?

This den lends itself perfectly to the outdoors. Ask permission to transform an existing shed into your den, or ask a DIY-savvy adult to help you build a permanent den with wood and recycled materials in a flat corner of a garden. It's great if you have some soil near the den that you can use for gardening, as well. But if you haven't got outdoor space available, don't panic! Instead, build yourself a recycled igloo that you can set up in a clear space indoors (see page 75).

DOWN ON THE FARM

You could ask an adult to help you transform a shed into a mini barn. Paint the shed in rustic colours such as red and orange for a true farmhouse feel.

INSPIRATION!

THE HEN-GINEERS

On the programme, this den was built to work for real egg-laying chickens. A chicken wire fence created a safe space for the hens, and the Dengineers even made a chicken flap for the birds to go in and out. Free range fun!

ENVIRONMENTALLY FRIENDLY

This eco den built on the programme was the perfect example of how rubbish can be reused and turned into something special. Made mainly of recycled materials, with a sloped roof to collect and reuse rainwater, and a living milk crate wall, it was friendly to the environment, too.

DENGINEERS' TOP TIP!

Think about how you could catch rainwater in your den to water your garden. - Tony and Satwinder

INSPIRATION!

LIVING WALL

Ask an adult to help you buy milk crates online. Fill each one with soil and plants. Stack the crates on top of each other in a cool coloured pattern to create a lush living wall.

MINIBEAST HOTEL

Provide a home for wildlife! The plants and soil in your milk crate wall double as a welcoming space for minibeasts. Place leaves, sticks and loose bark inside to create plenty of nooks and crannies for creepy-crawlies to get comfy.

FROM JUNK TO GEMS...

Make practical lovely items for your den out of no-longer-used objects found around your home.

DIY DESK

Turn unused wooden palettes into a desk for your den.

DOOR HANDLE HOOKS

Reusing old door handles is not only good recycling – it looks totally trendy too! Paint the door handles, then ask an adult to help you screw them into the wall to use as handy hooks.

TONS OF TUBES

Cardboard tubes are a great recycled material to collect. Save tubes from around your house or ask for unused empty tubes from fabric shops. Glue these vertically in place along the inner walls of your den for a fresh look. You could use them to make a photo frame, too!

TIN-CAN POTS

Carefully clean out old food tins and remove the labels. Paint the tins, then add soil and plant seeds or flowers inside.

POCKET STORAGE

With permission, cut the pockets out of old jeans. Glue or nail these to a particle board or your den's wall to create super-stylish storage for seeds, gardening tools and more.

BUILD AN ECO IGLOO

You could make your entire den structure out of reused plastic milk containers! You'll need to collect hundreds of these – rinse and dry out empty containers as you finish them. Ask friends and shops if you can have theirs too. To build an igloo, you'll also need cardboard boxes, craft tape, a glue gun and an adult to help.

1

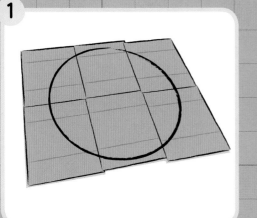

Unfold and flatten your cardboard boxes. Tape these into a square shape to create a cardboard base, the size you'd like your den to be. Draw a large circle on the base to show where your igloo will go.

2

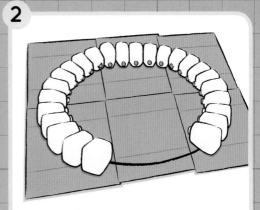

Lay milk containers flat on the circle, edges touching and caps facing inwards. Leave space for a door. Ask an adult to help you use the glue gun to join the containers together and stick them to the base. Leave to dry.

3

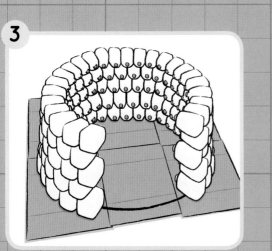

Glue another ring of containers on top of the first. Stagger each container in the new ring between the two containers in the ring below, as shown. Leave glue to dry. Repeat to create more rings, until you're happy with the height of your igloo. Leave the door space open on all rings.

4

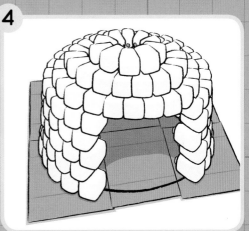

For the dome, create another ring of containers, this time placing each container in towards the centre slightly, so the walls start to arch over. Repeat until your rings meet at the top. For these rings, complete the full circle. Ask an adult to check that your igloo is sturdy and safe, then enjoy your eco dream den!

BEACH HUT DEN

HERE COMES THE SUN!

Are you always daydreaming of being at the beach? Bring your own little piece of paradise to your home or garden with this totally chilled-out Hawaiian hideaway.

WHERE TO BUILD?

This den is meant to be a Hawaiian haven, an escape from ordinary life. Tuck yours in wherever you can, but go all out with the beach vibe in whatever special spot you choose! If you have permission to transform an unused shed outside, you can create a permanent chill-out zone. Or, use a pop-up tent or cardboard structure in a sunny spot of your garden or house.

DENGINEERS' TOP TIP!

Think about including a canopy for shade. This will protect you from the sun and give you somewhere cooler to play. - Sege

JUICE BAR

Use a window in your den as your very own juice bar! Or, cut a hole in the side of a cardboard box big enough for you to sit in for a standalone serving place. Have cups and drink umbrellas at the ready for a sip of paradise.

BAMBOO

Bamboo is naturally waterproof, so it makes the perfect shelter. If you're building an outdoor den, find bamboo canes at a DIY shop to use for your roof and door.

INSPIRATION!

SANDY BEACH

If your den is outside, ask an adult to help you create a closed-in space using wood borders and a tarp lining, or find a premade sandbox or plastic paddling pool. Fill it with sand for your very own sandy beach!

DRIFTWOOD

You could cover your den's outer walls with planks of wood or strips of cardboard, to look like driftwood that was found on the beach. Paint these strips different colours for a bright and vibrant beachy den.

CAPTURE THE HAWAIIAN SPIRIT...

Try these tropical touches in your own beach den.

SURF'S UP

Fill your den with reminders of a tropical paradise: palm leaves, surfboards (real or made of cardboard!) and pineapples.

SUN AND SEA

Create the illusion of a sunset by the sea with clever paintwork. Paint straight on to the walls of your den, if you have permission, or on poster paper that you can stick to the wall and floor.

CHILL-OUT ZONE

It is super important to have somewhere to relax in this laid-back den. Bring in wicker chairs, sun loungers or just comfy cushions for a place to sit and chill.

MAKE A TIKI TOTEM POLE

Create a Tiki-inspired totem pole to sit outside your den. This perfect tropical touch is said to ward off evil... and maybe brothers and sisters too! Find some brown cardboard boxes and colourful paints, then go crazy!

1

TOP TIP: Traditionally, tikis have big open mouths.

With a pencil, draw expressive faces on each of your cardboard boxes. Get creative and try a different face on each one.

2

Paint each face using lots of bright colours. Leave to dry.

3

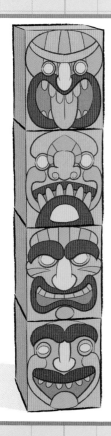

Stack the boxes on top of each other. Use tape to secure them in place. Place the totem pole outside your den for a Hawaiian welcome. Aloha!

OBSERVATORY

DEN

Explore the wonders of the universe with your very own mini observatory. Study science, space and the stars from this out-of-this-world den.

WHERE TO BUILD?

An observatory is a place to study space and look up into the starry night. Whether you build your den indoors or outdoors, make sure you choose somewhere with a clear view of the sky.

INDOOR DEN

An observatory in the comfort of your own home allows you a space where you can store all your stargazing kit. Start by choosing the best window in the house. This needs to give you the clearest and widest view of the night sky. Then build your den around this window. Use blankets, sheets or cardboard to create a dim space – the darker it is inside, the clearer you can see the stars shining outside!

OUTDOOR DEN

Get closer to nature by pitching a tent, hanging a tarp over a washing line or building a teepee out of large fallen branches (see pages 15 and 17). Make sure you leave a window for looking up at the stars! Don't forget to bring any equipment back inside when you're done for the night.

RAISE THE ROOF

If your den is outdoors, you could have a flap in the roof to look out at space when you want to - and keep the den dry and private the rest of the time!

INSPIRATION!

DEEP SPACE DECOR

Decorate the outside of your den with the night sky. Cut stars out of cardboard and paint them gold. Make 3D planets out of papier mâché. Glue these on to a background painted to look like galaxies.

HOW TO MAKE PAPIER MÂCHÉ PLANETS

1. Cut or tear newspaper into small strips.
2. In a bowl, mix a mug of flour with a mug of warm water. Stir until smooth. Add extra water, if needed.
3. Blow up a balloon. Paint the round end of the balloon with the flour paste and stick the newspaper strips on. Continue painting on paste and sticking on paper to cover a bowl-shaped section. Leave to dry.
4. Pop the balloon with a pin.
5. Paint the outside of the planet. Leave to dry.

DENGINEERS' TOP TIP!

Observatories usually have a full 360 degree view of the sky. Are there any trees near your den area? Do the branches stretch over to cover your view? Make sure you pick the clearest spot to see as much of the sky as possible.
- Maral

FOR THE ASPIRING ASTROPHYSICIST...

Try these ideas in your den to raise your stargazing game.

DISCOVERY STATION

Whether your den is indoors or outdoors, you'll need somewhere to note down any discoveries you make. This could be a desk or simply a notebook on your knee! Just make sure you keep a pen and pad in your den in case you discover the next big planet or solar system.

STAR CHARTS

Buy a poster from a shop or print out a star chart from the Internet. This can double as cool wallpaper for your den while also being an important reference for reading the night sky.

TELESCOPE

If you have a telescope, position it where it can point out the window of your den. Even better, place it on a circle of cardboard or thick plastic that you can rotate to aim the telescope at different parts of the sky.

UPCYCLE PROJECT! STARRY BLANKET

Wrap up in a cosmic blanket to keep cosy while watching the stars. Or, lay the blanket down as your den's floor to feel like you're in outer space yourself. Ask an adult for an old sheet or fleece (make sure it's been washed) and gather together some card, fabric paints and household sponges.

1

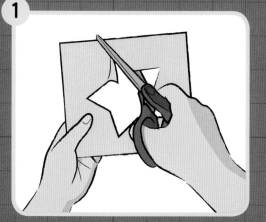

To make a stencil, draw a star on a piece of card. Carefully cut out the star, leaving the outer card intact.

2

Hold your stencil in place on the blanket or sheet. Dip a sponge in paint, then dab the sponge inside the stencil. Carefully peel back the stencil when the space is filled with paint.

3

Repeat step 2 to make a starry pattern on your blanket. Use different colours for the stars, if you like, and add as many as you want! Leave to dry before curling up with your creation.

BIGGEST DEN EVER

SUPERSIZE YOUR DEN!

Get together with a group of friends and build the most epic den ever! This is THE den for making memories with your mates.

WHERE TO BUILD?

This den needs to be somewhere you can all access. Find a large space in someone's garden (with permission), a clear room indoors or an open section of a neighbourhood park (but be sure to take away your things when you're done).

Here are two different ways you could build the biggest den ever...

1. A DEN OF MINI DENS

Your epic den could be made up of a load of mini ones. Try building and linking several cardboard caves or pop-up tents to create one ginormous dream den.

THEMED ROOMS

If you've got a space with several rooms, you could decorate each one differently for a den of many themes!

TENT PARTY

Have an epic slumber party with a pop-up tent den for each guest. Decorate the tents individually with different colours to suit your friends!

2. ONE MAHOOSIVE DEN

Ask an adult to help you and your friends create one giant den. This could be made of loads of cardboard boxes indoors or built with wood and nails outside. Either way, be sure your giant den is safe and won't fall down!

DENGINEERS' TOP TIP!

It's all about teamwork! This is a big den so make sure you have lots of help from people with different skills to bring your dream den together.
– Sege

TOWERING TREEHOUSE

Find a healthy, large tree and ask an adult who is good at building to help you build a treehouse with many levels and rooms.

INSPIRATION!

COOL CONNECTIONS

The Dengineers have built some epic community dens. They used pathways to connect multiple den buildings to make one massive den village.

MIX AND MATCH

The biggest den ever will be so mahoosive that you could have different areas for different activities: a place to hang out, a place to play, a place to party... and more! You could even combine some of the themes from this book into one multifunctioning mega den.

PARTY ZONE

Turn a section of your den (or one of your mini dens) into the party place! Stock it with party hats, props and lights for your next big event. Decorate the walls with bright colours. Don't forget to leave an open space for a dance floor!

INSPIRATION!

CHILL-OUT AREA

After all the partying and playing, you'll need a quiet place to hang out and chill with your friends. Fill a part of your den with beach-style lounge chairs, comfy bean bags or even luxurious cushions. Step up the relaxed vibe with your own library of shared books too!

SPORT SECTION

If you've got a large outdoor space available, you could create a multipurpose sports pitch and race track for group play. For your own version at home, ask an adult for permission and help to use special grass spray paint or chalk to mark the pitch and lanes.

Bring in chairs, blankets or benches for spectators to sit and cheer you on!

Make a large scoreboard using poster paper and markers.

MAKING MEMORIES

This den is all about you and your friends. So put yourselves on the walls, too! Use a corkboard or large poster paper to create a memories board where you can stick photos and crafts from your fun times together. Leave some blank space to add the new memories that you'll make in your epic den!

Sketching space

It's time to create! Sketch your dream den ideas and plans here. Be inspired by the theme suggestions in this book, or come up with your own!

Sketching space

DENGINEERS' TOP TIP!

Start with simple shapes and then add more detail.
Use different types of pens and different colours.
- Tony and Satwinder

Sketching space

Photo album

Show off your finished spaces! Take photos of the outside, inside and little details of your dens and paste them here.

THIS DEN IS
DONE!

WITH SPECIAL THANKS TO:

Sege Rosella, Maral Tulip, Emma Kosh, Satwinder Samra, Tony Broomhead, Lauren Layfield, Joe Tracini, Jennifer Morrison, Joanne Redfern and Annette Williams